SUNDAY SCHOOL
Matters

12 Matters that Matter to Your Church

Edited by

ALLAN TAYLOR

LifeWay Press®
Nashville, Tennessee

Published by LifeWay Press® • © 2016 Allan Taylor

No part of this book may be reproduced or transmitted in any form or by any means, electronic or mechanical, including photocopying and recording, or by any information storage or retrieval system, except as may be expressly permitted in writing by the publisher. Requests for permission should be addressed in writing to LifeWay Press®; One LifeWay Plaza; Nashville, TN 37234-0152.

ISBN 978-1-4300-6663-7 • Item 005792620

Dewey decimal classification: 268.1
Subject headings: SUNDAY SCHOOLS—ADMINISTRATION \
SUNDAY SCHOOLS—GROWTH

Scripture quotations marked HCSB are taken from the Holman Christian Standard Bible®, Copyright © 1999, 2000, 2002, 2003, 2009 by Holman Bible Publishers. Used by permission. Holman Christian Standard Bible®, Holman CSB®, and HCSB® are federally registered trademarks of Holman Bible Publishers. Scripture quotations marked NKJV are taken from the New King James Version. Copyright © 1979, 1980, 1982, Thomas Nelson Inc., Publishers. Scripture quotations marked NASB are taken from the New American Standard Bible®, Copyright © 1960, 1962, 1963, 1968, 1971, 1972, 1973, 1975, 1977, 1995 by The Lockman Foundation. Used by permission. (lockman.org) Scripture quotations marked KJV are taken from the King James Version.

To order additional copies of this resource, write to LifeWay Resources Customer Service; One LifeWay Plaza; Nashville, TN 37234-0113; fax 615.251.5933; call toll free 800.458.2772; order online at lifeway.com; email orderentry@lifeway.com; or visit the LifeWay Christian Store serving you.

Printed in the United States of America

Groups Ministry Publishing • LifeWay Resources
One LifeWay Plaza • Nashville, TN 37234-0152

CONTENTS

THE AUTHORS

ALLAN TAYLOR

Director, Church Education Ministry
LifeWay Christian Resources
Nashville, Tennessee

DAVID FRANCIS

Director, Sunday School
LifeWay Christian Resources
Nashville, Tennessee

BOB MAYFIELD

Sunday School and Small-Groups Specialist
Baptist General Convention of Oklahoma
Oklahoma City, Oklahoma

KEN COLEY

Professor of Christian Education
and Director of EdD Studies
Southeastern Baptist Theological Seminary
Wake Forest, North Carolina

ERIC GEIGER

Vice President, Resources Division
LifeWay Christian Resources
Nashville, Tennessee

DAN COOK

Minister of Education
Spotswood Baptist Church
Fredericksburg, Virginia

BEN PRITCHETT

Minister of Education
First Baptist Church
Houston, Texas

EUGENE MCCORMICK

Minister of Christian Education
Shiloh Metropolitan Baptist Church
Jacksonville, Florida

THOM RAINER

President and Chief Executive Officer
LifeWay Christian Resources
Nashville, Tennessee

CARTER SHOTWELL

Executive Pastor of Ministries
Lake Pointe Church
Rockwall, Texas

BRUCE RALEY

Executive Pastor
First Baptist Church
Hendersonville, Tennessee

HOW TO USE THIS RESOURCE

The following tips will help you maximize the effectiveness of this Sunday School training resource.

The title of this resource is *Sunday School Matters*. If you don't make the effort to conduct this 12-session training with intentionality, preparation, and enthusiasm, you've already sent the signal that Sunday School doesn't matter. Remember:

- Sunday School matters!
- This training resource matters!
- The training and edification of your leaders matter!
- So conduct this time as if it matters!

Sunday School matters so much that a church must have a proper enlistment of the leaders who matter most—teachers. James 3:1 instructs, "Not many should become teachers, my brothers, knowing that we will receive a stricter judgment" (HCSB). The Word of God places a higher standard on those who teach the Bible. On page 9 you'll find a suggested Sunday School teacher commitment that you can use to enlist teachers. Over time you can change your Sunday School one committed teacher at a time.

PREPLANNING

1. Promote the schedule and participation in this training weeks in advance.

2. Promote this training in the church bulletin, on the church website, by email, and during worship-service announcements.

3. Invite all Sunday School leaders through personal contacts.

4. Invite all potential Sunday School leaders through personal contacts.

5. Schedule one hour for each session—30 minutes to view the video teaching and 30 minutes to follow up with discussion and application, using the questions and exercises in each session of this study guide.

6. Make sure you're prepared to apply the principles from each session to your Sunday School by using the "Drive It Home" portion of each session in this study guide.

7. Make sure everyone has a study guide. Following along and filling in the blanks during the video session will keep each participant engaged in the teaching and will provide a resource for future reference.

8. Have pens available.

MEETING ROOM

1. Reserve a room for each session. It's best to use the same space each time.

2. Have comfortable chairs and arrange them so that everyone can clearly see the screen(s).

3. Show the sessions on a screen or screens large enough for everyone to see. Make sure the sound is adequate for the room size.

4. Make sure the room temperature is comfortable.

5. We don't encourage eating while viewing the sessions. This will distract learners and minimize the effectiveness of the sessions. We recommend a gathering time before the sessions for food and fellowship.

SETTINGS

This training can be offered in a variety of settings.

1. During regularly scheduled Sunday School leadership meetings

2. All day Saturday

3. Friday evening through Saturday

4. 12 consecutive Wednesday nights

5. 12 consecutive Sunday afternoons or nights

6. 12 consecutive Sunday mornings before other scheduled services and activities

7. A retreat setting

8. Because Sunday School is the way many congregations do church, offer the training for the whole church on Wednesday or Sunday evenings.

9. We don't recommend individual viewing of the video sessions. Group viewing and discussion build synergy, camaraderie, and teamwork. Everyone can share and build on others' knowledge and experience. Sharing the same point of reference builds accountability into the leader's application points.

SUNDAY SCHOOL TEACHER COMMITMENT

Carefully and prayerfully read the following teacher commitment. Respond by writing yes or no after each statement. Sign and date if you wish to join a team of leaders who are committed to minister to people and carry out the Great Commission through Sunday School.

1. I have a personal relationship with Jesus Christ.
2. I feel called by God to serve Him through the Sunday School.
3. I will strive to follow the leadership of the Holy Spirit.
4. I will be committed to the inerrancy of Scripture and to the doctrine of the church.
5. I will conduct my life in a manner that is above reproach.
6. I will be committed to teach with excellence through both preparation and presentation.
7. I will participate in training and growing opportunities.
8. I will participate in Sunday School leadership meetings.
9. I will personally engage with lost and unchurched people and will lead my class to do so.
10. I will do all I can to create a class that is loving, inviting, accepting, and friendly to all.
11. I will be faithful in tithing 10 percent of my gross income.
12. I will completely abstain from alcoholic beverages.
13. I will be faithful in attending the church's worship services.
14. I will support the pastor and staff.
15. I will strive to begin a new class every two years.
16. Before my Lord Jesus Christ, I commit to serve Him and His church by faithfully ministering through Sunday School.

_____
SIGNED

_____
DATE

SESSION 1

LEADERSHIP
Matters

Leadership is the most important factor in Sunday School! Nothing matters beyond the point where the leader takes it. If Sunday School is to *matter* in your church, then it must *matter* to those who lead it.

Verse that Matters

He [David] shepherded them with a pure heart
and guided them with his skillful hands.

PSALM 78:72, HCSB

WHY LEADERSHIP MATTERS
Statement that Matters

Your leadership is perfectly designed
to produce the results you're getting![1]

- When you design your leadership, you design your ministry. Your leadership is the blueprint of the ministry you are building.

Sunday School shoulders a tremendous ministry load for your church and is the Great Commission arm of the church. But all this work will go undone if we do not have proper leadership.

Tasks aren't self-sustaining; they all depend on someone to execute them faithfully, responsibly, specifically, and passionately.

THE WHAT AND HOW OF LEADERSHIP

1. What do leaders do? Leaders _____.

   A. Leaders are _____.

   > In the NFL you don't throw to open receivers; you throw receivers open.
   > STEVE YOUNG, HALL OF FAME QUARTERBACK

   Conformist   Catalyst   Rebel

   B. Leaders take the ministry to a _____ level.

      - Leaders refuse to accept _____.
      - Jesus isn't the _____ _____ for mediocrity.

2. What do leaders do? Leaders are _____.

   A. Vision drives everything.

   B. Leaders are _____.

      - The height of your doing will never _____ the height of your thinking.
      - Leaders think _____.

3. What do leaders do? Leaders _____.

   A. Leaders are _____-_____.

Status-quo statement: "We shall not be moved."

Leadership statement: "I will move."

- Jesus didn't follow the crowd; He led it. Jesus didn't report the news; He made it.

B. Leaders are _____ _____.

How do you change a mediocre Sunday School?

- Set enlistment standards. You cannot build a great Sunday School with uncommitted leaders (see Jas. 3:1). "Sunday School Teacher Commitment" (p. 9) is a helpful enlistment tool that provides key leadership standards.
- Surround yourself with godly advisers (see Prov. 15:22).
- Understand that change comes in small increments: one person at a time, one meeting at a time, one training session at a time, and one conversation at a time.
- Come to grips with your own biblical convictions, vision, and strategy for Sunday School, because nothing will *matter* until it first *matters* to you.

4. What do leaders do? Leaders _____.

A. Leaders possess a strong threefold cord: burden, conviction, and passion.

B. Leadership never rises from a vacuum; it rises from a _____ in the soul.

C. Leaders are willing to pay the price ... and it will cost.

- Leaders must go the _____ _____.

D. Every next level of your Sunday School will demand
a _____ _____ of you.

DRIVE IT HOME

1. How would you rate the effectiveness of your Sunday School ministry? Mark a number on the scale. Why did you rate your Sunday School that way?

   Weak   1   2   3   4   5   Strong

2. Does your rating reflect your leadership? How?

3. Where would you place yourself on the conformist-catalyst-rebel continuum?

4. As a leader, do you have a vision for your Sunday School? If so, can you write it? Read and discuss Habakkuk 2:2.

5. What areas of your Sunday School are strong? Why?

6. What areas of your Sunday School are weak? Why?

7. In what areas has mediocrity been tolerated?

8. What one area will you take the initiative to improve?

9. Do your Sunday School leaders know the purpose of Sunday School? Do your Sunday School leaders communicate that purpose to others?

10. How can your Sunday School leadership team design a Sunday School that produces the results you desire?

1. Adapted from Tom Northup, as quoted in "101 Inspiring Leadership Quotes," *resourcefulmanager* [online, cited 31 August 2016]. Available from the Internet: *resourcefulmanager.com*.

SESSION 2

VISION
Matters

If leadership is the most important factor in Sunday School, vision is perhaps the most important aspect of leadership. An effective leader rallies people to work with energy and in harmony to accomplish something. If that something is significant, it's fueled by vision. Paul expressed a 20:20 vision that could apply to Sunday School.

Verse that Matters

I did not shrink back from proclaiming to you anything that was profitable or from teaching it to you in public and from house to house.

ACTS 20:20, HCSB

WHY VISION MATTERS
Statement that Matters

Vision without action is a daydream.
Action without vision is a nightmare.[1]

JAPANESE PROVERB

- What you _____ is more important than what you _____.
- What you say is only as powerful as what you _____.

Sunday School leaders are the heirs of a movement _____ by vision historically and _____ by vision today.

THE WHAT AND HOW OF VISION

1. Vision lets you _____ more than you see.

   - Vision lets you see _____ _____.
   - Vision opens the window to what is _____.
   - Vision reveals what is possible with _____ _____.

2. Vision focuses _____.

   - Reaching people
   - Teaching people
   - Ministering to and with people

3. Vision empowers _____.

   - Expect _____ people _____ week.
   - Expect a great Bible study experience _____ week.
   - Expect people to say _____.

4. Vision is a source of _____.

   - Vision points to a _____ when you get off track.
   - Vision provides _____ when your speech falters.
   - Vision supplies _____ when you want to quit.

5. Vision is tested at the _____.

- The _____ from the door
- The _____ at the door
- The _____ out the door
- The _____ at their door

DRIVE IT HOME

1. You're the first person to arrive at the door of the room where your Sunday School class meets.

   - What do you see that is?
   - What do you see that you could probably change? Why?
   - What do you see that could happen only if God helped?

2. How are the priorities of Sunday School expressed in your church? Do they parallel reaching-teaching-ministering?

   Rearrange the three words on each line below to match the priorities of reaching-teaching-ministering.

Commission	Make disciples	Discover
Class	Build community	Connect
Community	Impact culture	Invite

   What would happen if your class got serious about all three of these priorities in your class? In your church?

3. What are some boundaries to your vision, based on the three priorities of Sunday School?

4. Do you expect new people every week? Does the class? How do you know? How would a new person know?

NOTES

1. Japanese proverb, *Thinkexist.com* [online, cited 25 August 2016]. Available from the Internet: *thinkexist.com*.

SESSION 3

SOULS Matter

Evangelism is Sunday School's lost priority! Bringing the lost to God was Jesus' primary ministry purpose. For followers of Christ, sharing the gospel with the lost is essential to Christ's lordship in our lives.

Verse that Matters

"Follow Me," Jesus told them, "and I will make you fish for people!"

MARK 1:17, HCSB

WHY SOULS MATTER
Statement that Matters

Souls *matter* to us because lost souls *matter* to God.

Luke 19:10	1 Timothy 1:15	1 Peter 3:18
John 3:16	Acts 4:12	Romans 5:8
Romans 1:16	1 Corinthians 1:18	

WHY EVANGELISM BELONGS IN SUNDAY SCHOOL
Three Arenas of Evangelism

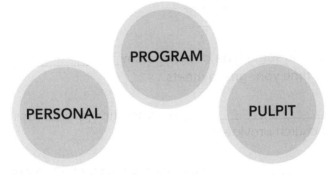

- Sunday School is the church's largest organization, and it makes sense the largest organization is focused on the church's _____ _____.

HOW TO BUILD A CULTURE OF EVANGELISM IN YOUR SUNDAY SCHOOL

1. Have a _____.

2. _____ the evangelism engagement of your group.

   Multiplier
   Lifestyle soul-winner
   Apprentice
   Gospel expression
   Testimony
   Inviters
   Spiritually aware
   Unengaged

3. Keep it _____ and _____.

4. Engage people where they are and move them forward.

3—_____

1—_____

5—_____

1—_____

5. Always do some type of evangelism _____ every time your group meets.

6. _____ evangelistic opportunities your church provides.

7. _____ an outreach plan for your group.

8. People follow their leader. Be a soul-winner yourself.

DRIVE IT HOME

1. How evangelistically engaged is your Sunday School class? Circle a number on the scale. What evidence supports your rating?

   Weak   1   2   3   4   5   Strong

2. Using the diagram "Three Arenas of Evangelism" (p. 19), draw each of the three circles in proportion to the number of people who were baptized in your church last year. How does knowing the three arenas affect your view of evangelism in the church?

3. Read Mark 1:17 and respond to the comment in the video about Jesus' ultimate aim for His group to be soul-winners. Do you agree or disagree? Why?

4. Identify how many people on your roll or ministry list may be lost. What's your plan to share the gospel with them?

5. How many lost people does your group know? Give group members 60 seconds to make a mark on a card for every lost person they know personally. Then total the numbers.

6. Can your class members take their Bible, sit down with unbelievers, and lead them to Jesus? If not, have your class members truly been discipled? What will you personally do to lead your Sunday School to become a group of soul-winners?

NOTES

SESSION 4

TEACHING Matters

Verses that Matter

This is why we constantly thank God, because when you received the message about God that you heard from us, you welcomed it not as a human message, but as it truly is, the message of God, which also works effectively in you believers.

1 THESSALONIANS 2:13, HCSB

We proclaim Him, warning and teaching everyone with all wisdom, so that we may present everyone mature in Christ. I labor for this, striving with His strength that works powerfully in me.

COLOSSIANS 1:28-29, HCSB

WHY TEACHING MATTERS

Statement that Matters

Effective Sunday School teachers guide their classes to focus on God's Word and strive for 100 percent engagement among their class members. When the class is actively engaged, learners experience increased comprehension and retain more of the content presented during the instructional episode.

Educational terms related to engagement:

- *Schema*
- *Differentiation*
- *Active learning*
- *Scaffolding*
- *Formative assessment*

Jesus engaged His learners on every page of the Gospels.

1. Jesus _____ the new ideas of the lesson with His learners' prior learning and experience.

2. Jesus _____ His learners in discussions in order to correct their thinking and to help them construct new understanding.

3. Jesus used a _____ of techniques to meet the needs of His learners.

4. Jesus modeled _____ learning techniques that lead to greater memory storage and retention.

5. Jesus _____ His learners' level of understanding.

6. Jesus _____ a focus on conviction and application.

Levels of engagement and modes of response: the goal is 100 percent engagement.

- *Thinking.* Ask your class to reflect on a recent situation or consider alternatives.
- *Reading.* Ask class members to look for or listen for a particular concept or fact found in the verses as the passage is read (aloud or silently). Never ask

members to read a passage without describing a specific idea for which they should look.

- *Writing.* Ask members to put ideas in their own words. Writing greatly increases engagement with the text and the likelihood of memory retention. The result need not be tightly organized or grammatically precise. Distribute note cards and consider collecting their responses.
- *Discussing.* Think-pair-share gives everyone the chance to talk without feeling intimidated by a teacher or a large group.
- *Cooperative learning.* Design a task that's clear and doable in a brief time period. Assign participants to groups in which each person has an assigned task. The assigned task includes a work product, and the group is held accountable for completing it.

Full group interaction and movement:

- *Gallery walk.* Groups present a final product that's hung like art in a gallery.
- *Graffiti wall.* Students write random responses on the board or on easel paper.

DRIVE IT HOME

1. What's the current level of engagement in your Sunday School class?

    - To what extent do class members participate? Circle a percentage.
      0%   25%   50%   75%   100%

    - Do you craft questions and engagement activities as you plan? Why or why not?

- Have you created an environment in which your members feel comfortable participating?

2. Rate your level of success with connecting your ideas to members' schema. Circle one.

   Don't try   Seldom   Occasionally   Often   Always

   - Why did you select that response?
   - What active-learning techniques could you use to increase engagement and get to know your group better?

3. What has your experience been with cooperative-learning groups? Share both positive and negative aspects of this approach.

4. Collaborate with your fellow teachers and design a cooperative-learning activity that would take five minutes or less.

5. How do you know whether your students are comprehending the focal passage?

   - Design some brief, quick formative-assessment activities that will provide you with valuable feedback about what members are thinking. Share your assessment ideas with your fellow teachers and solicit their feedback.

6. Examine John 4:7-30. Identify at least three teaching concepts that emerge from Jesus' conversation with the Samaritan woman at the well.

SESSION 5
TRANSFORMATION
Matters

The reason we serve and minister is to see transformed lives. How do we know if someone's life is really being transformed?

The supreme proof of a true conversion is holy affections, zeal for holy things, longings after God, longings after holiness, desires for purity.[1]
JONATHAN EDWARDS

Transformation is seeing the longing of the heart changed. It's hating what you once loved. Sin no longer tastes good.

WHY TRANSFORMATION MATTERS
Verses that Matter

Now the Lord is the Spirit, and where the Spirit of the Lord is, there is freedom. We all, with unveiled faces, are looking as in a mirror at the glory of the Lord and are being transformed into the same image from glory to glory; this is from the Lord who is the Spirit.

2 CORINTHIANS 3:17-18, HCSB

- Moses was changed by the _____ of God.

- Transformation happens in your class as you lead people to _____ Jesus more and more.

FRAMEWORK OF PERSONAL DISCIPLESHIP

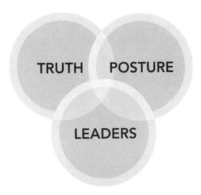

Statement that Matters

People are likely to be transformed when they encounter the truth of God through healthy leaders while they are in a teachable posture (the transformational sweet spot).

- Discipleship is not merely biblical information.

Churches that are transformational in discipleship help people encounter Jesus as Lord and not merely as Rabbi.[2]
ERIC GEIGER, MICHAEL KELLEY, AND PHILIP NATION

- Discipleship is not merely behavioral modification.

If a church views discipleship as merely tweaking behavior, then their work is contrary to the content of the gospel and the way of Jesus. Go after hearts. God does not desire to tweak our behavior. He desires to transform our lives.[3]
ERIC GEIGER, MICHAEL KELLEY, AND PHILIP NATION

- Discipleship is spiritual transformation.

1. Christian faith is _____ as much as it is taught.

2. Stir up your own _____ for Jesus.

3. _____ people to the author and the perfecter of their faith (see Heb. 12:2).

4. Sunday School classes put people in a _____ conducive for transformation.

5. "The research is compelling; God is using groups to bring about transformation in the lives of His people."[4] —Ed Stetzer and Eric Geiger

   The research revealed eight areas:

Bible engagement	Obeying God and denying self
Serving God and others	Sharing Christ
Exercising faith	Seeking God
Building relationships	Unashamed (transparency)

DRIVE IT HOME

1. In your honest opinion is your Sunday School more interested in people's attendance than in their spiritual transformation?

2. In your honest opinion is your Sunday School more interested in members' Bible knowledge than in their likeness to Jesus?

3. In your honest opinion is your Sunday School class a conducive environment for people to grow spiritually? In what ways?

4. Which of the following are you seeing most in your group members (check one)? Why?

___ Biblical information

___ Behavioral modification

___ Spiritual transformation

5. Rate your class by assigning a number to each statement below. Let 1 represent low and 5 high.

___ The truth of God's Word is taught in our group.

___ Our group has healthy spiritual leaders.

___ Our group is a conducive environment for growth.

6. Why don't we see more transformation in the lives of our Sunday School members?

7. Read John 14:15,21,23; James 1:22-25; 4:17; Romans 12:1-2.

- Discuss what these Scriptures teach about spiritual transformation.
- Discuss ways your Sunday School can better lead people to be spiritually transformed.

NOTES

1. Jonathan Edwards, as quoted in Eric Geiger, Michael Kelley, and Philip Nation, *Transformational Discipleship* (Nashville: B&H, 2012), 29.
2. Eric Geiger, Michael Kelley, and Philip Nation, *Transformational Discipleship*, 20.
3. Ibid., 28.
4. Ed Stetzer and Eric Geiger, *Transformational Groups* (Nashville: B&H, 2014), 39.

SESSION 6

CURRICULUM
Matters

Good curriculum is vital to the health of your Sunday School. Curriculum is the GPS (global-positioning system) guiding a church's journey in spiritual transformation. It sets the goal of what the church wants its members to know. Without curriculum your church is on a journey to nowhere. If you aim at nothing, you'll hit it every time. If Sunday School is to *matter* in your church, then focused attention should be given to the curriculum that is being utilized.

Definition that Matters

Curriculum is a strategic plan for the teaching of your Sunday School members through a systematic and comprehensive study of God's Word.

Verse that Matters

All Scripture is inspired by God and is profitable for teaching, for rebuking, for correcting, for training in righteousness.

2 TIMOTHY 3:16, HCSB

WHY CURRICULUM MATTERS
Statement that Matters

Your curriculum or lack of curriculum is taking your Sunday School in a certain direction. You better like the destination!

1. _____ teaching: good curriculum ensures a balanced treatment of God's Word.

2. Class _____: good curriculum encourages class members to prepare for class participation.

3. _____ of leaders: good curriculum makes enlisting and apprenticing teachers easier.

4. _____ of lesson: good curriculum helps learners apply what they learn on Sunday to their Monday morning.

5. _____ of groups: good curriculum keeps the classes open and focused outward.

   • There are few things that will close a class quicker than curriculum.

THE WHAT AND HOW OF CURRICULUM

1. _____ sound: make sure the curriculum is biblically accurate.

2. _____ sound: make sure the curriculum has a balanced scope and sequence.

   • The word *curriculum* comes from a Latin word meaning *a race course*. It shares the same root as the English word *current*, which speaks of the flow of water in a stream or an ocean current.

3. _____ sound: make sure
the curriculum is focused on application.

- As a Sunday School teacher teaches the lesson,
  they should visualize a question mark above every
  student's head. That question mark represents the
  question they're all asking: *What does this have
  to do with my Monday morning?*

4. _____ sound: make sure
the curriculum encourages various teaching methods.

- Learning is accomplished best when the learner
  is involved.
- Good curriculum includes a solid teaching plan, good
  discussion questions, meaningful learning activities,
  and practical ideas for application.
- People can't apply what they've not first learned.
  People cannot learn what they don't first understand.

5. _____ sound: make sure the curriculum
is easy to use.

6. _____ sound: make sure
the curriculum promotes an open-group philosophy.

- The wrong curriculum can close a group as quickly
  as a lack of space or an inward-focused class.

7. _____ sound: make sure the curriculum
is affordable.

DRIVE IT HOME

Evaluate your present Sunday School curriculum by answering the following questions.

1. Is it doctrinally sound? Does it have a balanced approach for covering Scripture? Does it address difficult passages in the Bible?

2. Is it directionally sound? What are the scope and sequence for this curriculum? Is this the path of learning you want your Sunday School members to travel?

3. Is it educationally sound? How much of each lesson is focused on application? Does each lesson have a clear lesson aim?

4. Is it methodologically sound? Does it include a solid teaching plan, good discussion questions, meaningful learning activities, and practical ideas for application?

5. Is it practically sound? How easy or difficult is it for teachers to prepare a lesson? What teacher helps are provided?

6. Is it philosophically sound? Does it allow students to enroll in the group at any time during the study?

7. It is financially sound? Is it affordable?

NOTES

SESSION 7

MINISTRY
Matters

One of the most basic and Christlike tasks of the Sunday School is the opportunity to minister to one another in Christ's name. The Sunday School class enrollment provides a ministry list of those in the body assigned to us for whom we are to care.

Verse that Matters

By this all men will know that you are My disciples, if you have love for one another.

JOHN 13:35, NASB

WHY MINISTRY MATTERS
Statement that Matters

One of the most important benefits for being in a Sunday School class is the realization that others care for you and are there to prayerfully help you in a time of need.

- We build a strong bond and spiritual relationship when we touch others by caring for them through our ministry. This expression of love provides a clear witness that we are His disciples.

In most churches the Sunday School almost always provides the first ministry touch when class members or their families confront a crisis. This act of ministry strengthens those who give, as well as those who receive. It's a clear reflection of Christ's love for all of His children.

THE WHAT AND HOW OF MINISTRY

1. Place a high _____ on ministry.

   - Lead your class to make a _____ to ministry.
   - Communicate to your members the _____.

   > Therefore, as we have opportunity, we must work for the good of all, especially for those who belong to the household of faith.
   > GALATIANS 6:10, HCSB

2. Effective ministry is too much for one or two persons; it takes a _____.

   - Ask God to _____ the right members to the team.

   > Pray ye therefore the Lord of the harvest, that he will send forth labourers into his harvest.
   > MATTHEW 9:38, KJV

   - Actively _____ the members of this team.

3. Once the teams are enlisted, it is important to _____ and _____ them for the task.

- Provide members of the team with a _____ _____ laying out a clear understanding of their task and your expectation.
- When needed, provide new leaders with on-the-job training.

4. _____ _____ your care groups. Do not haphazardly put these teams together.

   - A good group should include a _____ of *regular* attenders, *frequent* attenders, and *occasional* attenders. This gives each care group needed workers and spreads the workload among all care groups.
   - Each group should also _____ those on roll who never or seldom attend.

5. Hold your care groups accountable for their work.

   - If you never hold them accountable, you send a message that this task is _____ _____ .

6. Encourage your care groups to meet at least once a month to build _____ within the class and an openness for members to share their needs.

DRIVE IT HOME

1. How important do you feel personal ministry to class members is to effective Sunday School ministry? Circle a number on the scale. Why did you answer this way?

   Low   1   2   3   4   5   High

2. Is this an area in which your Sunday School is strong or weak? Why?

3. What would need to change to strengthen the ministry happening in your Sunday School?

4. Are your Adult Sunday School classes set up with care groups that minister to members?

5. What way(s) do you feel that ministering to members through your Sunday School helps build community in your class?

6. What are some ways meeting with your care group during the month can enhance this ministry?

7. In what ways does personally ministering to your class members reflect the love of Christ?

NOTES

SESSION 8

ORGANIZATION

Matters

Mastering foundational principles of effective Sunday School organization is paramount for all leaders of educational ministry. Order and organization must always be the first strategic priority.

Verse that Matters

But everything must be done decently and in order.

1 CORINTHIANS 14:40, HCSB

WHY ORGANIZATION MATTERS

Statement that Matters

Organizing is what you do before you do something, so that when you do it, it is not all mixed up.[1]

A. A. MILNE

- For any model or concept of ministry to be successful, a solid infrastructure must be firmly set in place. Infrastructure is the central foundation, the underlying architecture of any system or organization that determines how well it functions.

Structure should precede strategy. Before a strong Sunday School ministry can be built, it is imperative to know what its structure should look like. The principle is very similar to that of building a home. Before one starts to build, one must first develop a set of blueprints. Blueprints help determine what is to be built, how it is to be built, and where it is to be built. As one parallels the idea of why blueprints *matter* to the perspective of why organization *matters*, it becomes imperative to define, design, and direct the structure of Sunday School ministry.

THE WHAT AND HOW OF ORGANIZATION

1. Defining the Structure of Sunday School Ministry

   - Clearly define the _____ of the ministry.

   If you don't see it before you see it, you will never see it.[2]
   JOHNNY HUNT

   - Clearly define the _____ of the ministry.

   If you don't know where you are,
   you can't get where you're going.[3]
   SCOTT SCHWERTLY

   - Clearly define the _____ of the ministry.

   If you don't know where you are going,
   any road will take you there.[4]
   LEWIS CARROLL

2. Designing the Structure of Sunday School Ministry

   - Secure the vocal and visible support of the
     _____.

- Organize a strong but diversified leadership team.
- Develop ministry descriptions for all service positions.
- Establish parameters for teacher-learner _____, class _____ and composition, and starting _____ units.
- Exercise sound decision making in _____ selection.

3. Directing the Structure of Sunday School Ministry

   - Incorporate the _____ components of reaching, teaching, and ministering into the infrastructure of the ministry.
   - Develop an ongoing process of _____ and _____ teachers and volunteers for the ministry.
   - Maintain the essential _____ of communication, motivation, and delegation (inform, inspire, involve).
   - Adopt effective _____ processes (planning, budgeting, reports, evaluation, etc.).
   - Cultivate and constantly nurture strategic _____ with teachers, volunteers, and other key church leadership.
   - Review and identify the needs of the people and ministry regularly.

DRIVE IT HOME

1. What does the present organizational structure of your Sunday School ministry look like?

2. How is the existing organizational structure of your Sunday School ministry meeting current needs?

3. What challenges currently exist that might hinder improving the structure of your Sunday School ministry?

4. What's one strategy that can be immediately implemented to *define* the structure of Sunday School ministry?

5. What's one strategy that can be immediately implemented to *design* the structure of Sunday School ministry?

6. What's one strategy that can be immediately implemented to *direct* the structure of Sunday School ministry?

7. How can you better organize your Sunday School to reach people, teach people, and minister to people?

NOTES

1. A. A. Milne, as quoted in Lisa Montanaro, *The Ultimate Life Organizer* (White Plains, NY: Peter Pauper, 2011), 6.
2. Johnny Hunt, as quoted in Fred K. Hutto, *The Pattern* (Maitland, FL: Xulon, 2011), 141.
3. Scott Schwertly, *Ethos 3* [online], 18 October 2013 [cited 24 August 2016]. Available from the Internet: *ethos3.com*.
4. Lewis Carroll, *NotableQuotes* [online, cited 24 August 2016]. Available from the Internet: *notable-quotes.com*.

SESSION 9
ASSIMILATION
Matters

Research has demonstrated that Sunday School is unrivaled in assimilating people into the churches. Churches have many wonderful activities, but none of them, including corporate worship, are as effective in getting people to stick as Sunday School.

Verses that Matter

So the body is not one part but many.
Now there are many parts, yet one body.
1 CORINTHIANS 12:14,20, HCSB

WHY ASSIMILATION MATTERS
Statement that Matters

The involvement of Sunday School is tantamount to effective assimilation. No other church ministry comes close in effectiveness as Sunday School in retaining members.

You Have an Assimilation Problem If …

1. You don't _____ church visitors.

2. Church attendance does not _____ proportionate to membership gains.

3. Members are becoming _____ involved.

KEY INGREDIENTS FOR EFFECTIVE SUNDAY SCHOOL ASSIMILATION

1. Sunday School is the _____ ministry of the church.

   A. Sunday School is how you _____ church.

   B. Remember, all ministries are not created equal. When Sunday School is neglected, the wide-open front door is often countered by a wide-open back door.

2. Sunday School is both the church's evangelism strategy and assimilation strategy. They work in _____.

   A. The way you reach them is the way you keep them.

   B. Never _____ your assimilation strategy from your evangelism strategy.

3. Sunday School is _____ in purpose.

   A. Sunday School must intentionally _____ after people, intentionally stay in _____ with people, and intentionally _____ for people's needs.

   B. Sunday School must intentionally _____ _____ with prospects and absentee members.

   C. An intentional Sunday School will see people assimilated in a group _____ they join the church.

4. Sunday School is properly _____.

   A. Assimilation is best accomplished in age-graded, homogeneous groups where people _____.

   B. A well-organized Sunday School is _____, integrating sound teaching, intentional evangelism, meeting people's needs, fellowship, and relationships.

   C. Simply put, Sunday School will work if you _____ it.

5. Preschool, Children, and Youth Sunday School is _____ in reaching and keeping young families.

   A. Young families often represent the most _____ demographic to the church as they seek spiritual training for their children.

B. Retaining young families requires diligence in four areas:
   (1) Professional, trained, and caring staff
   (2) Engaging Bible teaching
   (3) Safe environment
   (4) Clean facility

6. A new-members class is a highly effective assimilation tool.

   A. A new-members class is used as a point of _____ where expectations of membership are articulated.

   B. The most effective new-members classes are conducted on Sunday mornings or Sunday afternoons.

   C. Research shows that new-members classes are the _____ in high-assimilation churches.

DRIVE IT HOME

1. Discuss: Are you retaining people who visit your church and Sunday School? How do you intentionally greet and assist visitors? Do visitors return after their first visit? How are you following up with visitors?

2. Compare your average worship attendance with your average Sunday School attendance. How big is the gap between the two? What can be done to close the gap?

3. What steps are you taking to incorporate new members into Sunday School classes? How can you improve?

4. Is Sunday School the priority ministry of your church? Does it take precedence in the allocation of key leaders, budget, facility construction and use, resources, staff hiring, and so on?

5. Is Sunday School both your evangelism strategy and your assimilation strategy? Can this bond be improved? Which is weaker—evangelism or assimilation? How can it be strengthened?

6. Is your Sunday School properly organized and ready to receive new people? How can this improve?

7. Are your preschool, children's, and youth divisions well staffed? Do the leaders receive excellent training? Are the facilities appropriate for these areas of ministry?

8. Do you have a new-members class? If not, what would it take to start one? If so, is it effective?

NOTES

SESSION 10
GROWTH
Matters

The Great Commission compels us to reach, teach, baptize, and multiply. Growth is not an option. The early church began large and kept growing. We're to work to make as many disciples as possible, and a growing Sunday School is the most effective organization to accomplish this goal.

Verses that Matter

Those who accepted his message were baptized, and that day about 3,000 people were added to them. And every day the Lord added to them those who were being saved.

ACTS 2:41,47, HCSB

Statement that Matters

Spiritual and numerical growth go hand in hand. A spiritually mature person should understand the need to reach and disciple the lost. We live in the most connected yet disconnected time in history. People are starving for authentic relationships. The church must build a bridge to the lost, influence them where they are, and work to get them connected through the Sunday School.

THE EIGHT-STEP STRATEGY

1. Build relationships with the unchurched.

2. Know how to share your faith.

3. Invite people to church and Sunday School.

4. Attend worship.

5. Attend Sunday School.

6. Contribute by serving.

7. Contribute by giving.

8. Contribute by developing others.

THE WHAT AND HOW OF GROWTH

1. Common growth-barrier excuses:

   - Demographics
   - Limited space
   - No new leaders
   - Not enough time
   - Church location
   - No vision
   - Twenty-something unchurched
     do not want to come to church.

2. There are no space limitations; there's only limited
   _____.

3. Always be in new-start mode.

4. How to multiply your Sunday School

- Step 1: Make birthing a new class a _____ _____.
- Step 2: The leadership must maintain the vision for birthing new classes.
- Step 3: Look for _____ that your class needs to multiply.
- Step 4: Recognize that birthing a new class creates new leadership opportunities.
- Step 5: Use the _____ methods.

5. Go after the people.

6. A good first-impressions PLAN

- P_____: enlist hosts or hostesses who are warm and outgoing and who proactively serve your guests.
- L_____: lead guests where you want them to go.
- A_____: there should be a reliable team of hosts who will be in Sunday School on time and purposeful about meeting guests.
- N_____ _____: the process of welcoming a guest to your Sunday School should be systematic.

7. Demonstrate _____ crisis and chronic care.

8. _____ networking

9. Strategies for reaching the unchurched

- _____ outreach
- Capitalize on big days.
- _____ evangelism training.
- Provide quality children and student ministries.
- Hot-_____ classes
- Get-_____ campaigns

DRIVE IT HOME

1. Take five minutes in your group and record the first names of nonbelievers (such as family, neighbors, and work associates) with whom members are affiliated.

2. How many nonbelievers did your group discover?

3. How can members take the following steps to reach the lost?
   a. Build relationships with a nonbelievers.

   b. Share verbal witnesses.

   c. Invite nonbelievers to church.

4. How open and prepared is your class to reach and welcome nonbelievers?

5. What steps need to be taken for your class to be more open and prepared to reach and welcome nonbelievers?

6. Does your class have an "invite" mentality? Are your class members consistently inviting people to Sunday School?

7. New groups attract new people. What can your class do to help birth a new class or relaunch a class?

NOTES

SESSION 11

NEW GROUPS
Matter

Discipleship takes place best in the context of relationships. But where can those relationships develop in the church? The best place is in smaller groups. Your Sunday School is the place for people to connect. A new Sunday School group provides an even more likely place.

Verse that Matters

We proclaim Him, warning and teaching *everyone* with all wisdom, so that we may present *everyone* mature in Christ.
COLOSSIANS 1:28, HCSB, EMPHASIS ADDED

WHY NEW GROUPS MATTER
Statement that Matters

All of God's living, earthly creations are designed to reproduce. In fact, anything that doesn't reproduce becomes extinct. Even Sunday School groups have a lifespan. Therefore, each group should reproduce itself time and again.

THE WHAT AND HOW OF NEW GROUPS

1. New Sunday School classes help _____ the back door of your church.

   In most churches as many people are headed out the back door as are entering the front door. Reasons include:

   - A lack of relationships
   - No responsibility
   - Not much *new* in the group

2. New Sunday School classes _____ more people in ministry.

   - Each new group needs _____.
   - Additional leaders provide additional ministry _____.
   - _____ people are more likely to stick.

3. New Sunday School classes usually begin as _____ groups.

   - Open groups _____ new people every time they meet.
   - Factors in determining whether a group is open or closed: content, environment, attitude, intentionality
   - Unless highly intentional, open groups are prone to _____ at some point in time.
   - As relationships within the group _____, the group may become closed.

4. New Sunday School groups _____ on new people.

   - "God has placed each one of the parts in one body just as He wanted" (1 Cor. 12:18, HCSB).

- New groups usually have some sort
  of _____.
- People _____ others to that which is new.
- A diverse group can be a powerful, impacting group.

5. New Sunday School groups' foundation must be Bible study.

- While relationships are crucial in group ministry, the
  _____ _____ must be the Word of God.
- There is a _____ between
  a Bible study and a Bible-based study.

6. Barriers must be overcome in order to reproduce yourself.

- New groups must be started _____.
- New groups usually require a _____.
- Time and location must be determined.
- Existing groups have to be _____.
- _____ after the people.

Go, therefore, and make disciples of all nations,
baptizing them in the name of the Father and of the
Son and of the Holy Spirit, teaching them to observe
everything I have commanded you. And remember,
I am with you always, to the end of the age.
MATTHEW 28:19-20, HCSB, EMPHASIS ADDED

Begin new groups!

DRIVE IT HOME

1. Name people who are members of your Sunday School class
   but haven't attended in a while. Are there specific reasons
   for their lack of attendance?

2. Use the following questions to discuss whether your group is open or closed.

- Do your members regularly invite others?
- Do guests attend group fellowships?
- Have you reached at least two new members in the past six months?
- Are at least 20 percent of empty seats allotted for visitors?
- Do you have extra personal study guides for guests?
- Are guests quickly followed up after attending?
- Do guests attend a second or third time?
- Does your curriculum allow new people to understand the lesson without having a knowledge of prior content?

3. Identify groups of people who might have a difficult time breaking into the fellowship of your existing Sunday School groups.

4. What members of your Sunday School class possess the ability to lead groups of their own?

5. What barriers need to be overcome for your group to reproduce itself?

NOTES

SESSION 12

NOW

Matters

Now. It's all we've got. We can't recall yesterday. It's forever history, and tomorrow is not promised.

The great French marshal Hubert Lyautey once asked his gardener to plant a tree. The gardener objected that the tree would grow slowly and wouldn't reach maturity for one hundred years. The marshal replied, "In that case, there is no time to lose; plant it this afternoon!"[1]

Verses that Matter

So teach us to number our days, that
we may apply our hearts unto wisdom.
PSALM 90:12, KJV

I must work the works of Him who sent Me while
it is day; the night is coming when no one can work.
JOHN 9:4, NKJV

Do you not say, "There are still four months and then comes
the harvest"? Behold, I say to you, lift up your eyes and
look at the fields, for they are already white for harvest!
JOHN 4:35, NKJV

Walk in wisdom toward those who
are outside, redeeming the time.
COLOSSIANS 4:5, NKJV

WHY NOW MATTERS
Statement that Matters

In light of the current status of the American church,
now matters. In light of eternity, *now* matters.

	1990	Now
Total churches	37,974	46,499
Total baptisms	385,031	305,301
Baptisms per church per year	10	6.5
Baptisms per members	1 per 26	1 per 51
Baptisms per U.S. population	1 per 661	1 per 1,049
Sunday School attendance	3,851,340	3,723,679

Now there were four leprous men at the entrance
of the gate; and they said to one another,
"Why are we sitting here until we die?"
2 KINGS 7:3, NKJV

THE WHAT AND HOW OF *NOW*

1. You can't build a ministry on what you're going to do.

    - We are not measured by our _____;
      we are measured by our _____.
    - Drastic times _____ drastic measures.

   **One of the great mistakes is to judge policies and
   programs by their intentions rather than their results.[2]**
   MILTON FRIEDMAN

2. The longer you wait to reenergize a flawed Sunday School,
   the more _____ it becomes.

    - Your Sunday School can't be better tomorrow without
      doing something _____.
    - "Woe to them that are at ease in Zion" (Amos 6:1, KJV).

3. When we don't move with a sense of urgency, we …

    - _____ progress;
    - _____ productivity;
    - _____ status quo;
    - _____ opportunity.

4. Get started. Begin where you are.

    A. If you wait on perfect _____,
       you'll never do it.

    - Underachievers: "I won't do it until it's right."
    - Achievers: "I will do it until it's right."
    - "Go to the ant, you sluggard! Consider her ways
      and be wise" (Prov. 6:6, NKJV).

B. If you wait to get _____ on board, you'll never do it.

- Every significant movement will generate debate, if not opposition.
- The doors of opportunity at your church are marked _____.

5. Urgency is needed most when it is _____ least.

- The time to be right is when everyone else is wrong.
- The time to be burdened is when everyone else is at ease.
- The time to be convicted is when everyone else is apathetic.
- The time to be passionate is when everyone else is lethargic.
- The time to be concerned is when everyone else is complacent.
- The time to be focused is when everyone else is distracted.
- The time to lead is when everyone else is wandering.

6. Difficult places are _____ soil for great opportunity.

- Joseph did something great because he was sold as a slave.
- Moses did something great because his nation was in bondage.
- David did something great because there was a giant.
- Esther did something great because of planned Jewish extermination.
- Nehemiah did something great because Jerusalem was a reproach.
- Jesus did something great because there was sin.
- Paul did something great because people were lost.
- You can do something great because …

LET'S DO IT!

1. Difficulty—it's what God excels at, so take faith!

    - Little is much when God is in it.
    - "Is any thing too hard for the LORD?"
      (Gen. 18:14, KJV).
    - "There is nothing too hard for thee" (Jer. 32:17, KJV).
    - "With God all things are possible" (Matt. 19:26, NKJV).
    - "With God nothing will be impossible" (Luke 1:37, NKJV).

2. Difficulty—it's what God excels at, so take courage!

    - "Thus saith the LORD of hosts; let your hands
      be strong" (Zech. 8:9, KJV).
    - "The LORD spoke to Joshua …, saying, 'Be strong
      and of good courage. … Only be strong and very
      courageous. Have I not commanded you? Be strong
      and of good courage. Only be strong and of good
      courage' " (Josh. 1:1,6-7,9,18, NKJV).
    - "God has not given us the spirit of fear; but of power,
      and of love, and of a sound mind" (2 Tim. 1:7, KJV).
    - "There is no fear in love; but perfect love casts out
      fear" (1 John 4:18, NKJV).

If not you, who?
If not now, when?
If not in your church, if not in your Sunday School, whose?

DRIVE IT HOME

1. Be honest. Do you feel a sense of urgency for your church's
    Sunday School ministry? Why or why not?

2. Do your church and Sunday School leaders as a team feel
    a sense of urgency? If not, what's preventing this?

3. Is your Sunday School "at ease in Zion" (Amos 6:1, KJV)? Why or why not?

4. Read Matthew 24:42; 25:13. In light of the imminent return of Christ, should there be a sense of urgency in God's church?

5. Read Matthew 26:36-45. Jesus had a heavy heart and asked his inner circle to stay awake and watch with Him, but they fell asleep at the critical time when Jesus needed them. They fell asleep on their watch. Are we asleep on our watch?

6. Do the statistics shared in this session indicate that we're asleep on our watch? Does your answer grieve you? Burden you? Will it move you to do something about it?

7. Close this time with group prayer. Cry out to God and repent of any personal or corporate sins. Ask God to stir the Sunday School leadership team and to unite your hearts. Ask God to awaken your Sunday School and to do a fresh new work.

NOTES

1. Max Adams, *The Wisdom of Trees* (London: Head of Zeus, 2014).
2. Milton Friedman, as quoted in Ben Duronio, "Nine Unforgettable Quotes from Milton Friedman," *Business Insider* [online], 31 July 2012 [cited 25 August 2016]. Available from the Internet: businessinsider.com.

THE **BEST BIBLE STUDY** IS THE ONE THAT **FITS YOUR GROUP BEST.**